W9-BWI-916

Nellie Bly

A Name to Be Reckoned With

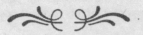

BY STEPHEN KRENSKY

ILLUSTRATED BY REBECCA GUAY

ALADDIN PAPERBACKS

New York   London   Toronto   Sydney   Singapore

First Aladdin Paperbacks edition July 2003
Text copyright © 2003 by Stephen Krensky
Illustrations copyright © 2003 by Rebecca Guay

ALADDIN PAPERBACKS
An imprint of Simon & Schuster Children's Publishing Division
1230 Avenue of the Americas
New York, NY 10020

Designed by Debra Sfetsios
The text of this book was set in Cheltenham.

Printed in the United States of America
2 4 6 8 10 9 7 5 3 1

Library of Congress Control Number 2002107412
ISBN 0-689-85573-7

For Susie Cohen

CHAPTER ONE

A Lucky Meeting

ONE WINTER DAY in 1885 a young woman stood on a downtown corner in Pittsburgh, Pennsylvania. The street was busy with horse-drawn wagons and people going about their business. The young woman hardly noticed. She had other things on her mind. And if she seemed a little nervous or hesitant, nobody stopped to stare.

The young woman's gaze was drawn to the imposing building in front of her. It was five stories high with a big flag waving from the top. She raised her eyes to the fourth floor. Behind those windows were the editorial offices of the Pittsburgh *Dispatch*, the well-known daily newspaper.

Maybe coming here had been a mistake. After all, she was only twenty-year-old Elizabeth Cochrane from the small town of Cochran's Mills, Pennsylvania. Her father had died when she was six, and she had never even finished high school. She lived with her mother and one sister in a row house where they took in boarders to help make ends meet. The family had been wealthy once, but those days were long past. And Pink, as Elizabeth was known, had spent the last four years in one dead-end job after another.

Then again, it was no accident that she was standing at this spot. The *Dispatch* had been publishing editorials making fun of women who wanted careers. "What Girls are Good For" ran one headline in the series.

The *Dispatch* writer was convinced that they were "restless" and "dissatisfied" for no good reason. What was their problem, anyway? Why couldn't girls understand that staying at home was best? They should get married, tend to their families, and stop all this nonsense about careers.

Pink hadn't liked that, not one bit. She might be only twenty years old, but she knew how it felt to be frustrated at work. She had nothing against everyday jobs for those who wanted them. But why should an enterprising woman's career be limited when a man's was not? Why should the only choice for a woman be marriage or a lowly job? Not every girl fit into such a neat package.

The truth was Pink already knew she wanted to be a writer. That was why she had written to the *Dispatch* after the editorial appeared. It felt good to get her thoughts down on paper even when they were angry ones. She had signed the letter, "Lonely Orphan Girl" and mailed it off.

The *Dispatch* had received a lot of letters about the editorials, but Lonely Orphan Girl's had stood out. In fact, the editor, George Madden, liked it so much that he posted a notice in the newspaper on January 17, inviting "Lonely Orphan Girl" to visit their offices.

And so here it was, January 18, the very next day, and Pink was standing outside in the cold. With her cheeks much the same color as her name, she finally got the courage to climb the stairs and announce herself.

The first meeting was a surprise for both sides. Pink expected to face a crusty old man as set in his chair as he was in his ways.

But here was a youngish fellow maybe ten years older than she was. As for George Madden, he hardly expected to find such bold writing coming from the pen of so shy and young a girl.

Still, Madden's instincts told him that Lonely Orphan Girl had something to offer. He wasn't going to print her letter, he explained. Instead he wanted to hire her to write an article for the newspaper. And who knew where that might lead?

Pink agreed to give it a try.

CHAPTER TWO

First Impressions

SINCE THE LONELY Orphan Girl spoke with such passion about the plight of women, George Madden told her to write more about it. So she did, and a week later the *Dispatch* published her first article—"The Girl Puzzle." In it Pink wrote about the unfavorable place women held in the business world. She explained that the "schools are overrun with teachers, the stores with clerks, the factories with employees. There are more cooks, chambermaids, and washerwomen than can find full employment." Should marriage be the only route these women could take to survive? Pink certainly didn't think so. "Take some girls that have the ability," she added, "procure for them situations. Pull them out of the mire and give them a shove up the ladder of life."

Her second article was about divorce, a familiar subject to Nellie because her own mother had divorced her third husband. Divorce was still rare, and the existing laws made it difficult to get—especially for a woman. The story raised a number of issues. In particular it clearly questioned the common wisdom of the day—that even a bad marriage was better than no marriage at all.

Madden was pleased with Pink's work, and he now asked her to join his staff. The position paid five dollars a week—more than any factory job a woman might get. All Pink needed now, he said, was the right name to write under. Her first piece had been credited to "Orphan Girl," but that wasn't a proper byline. Madden asked for suggestions in the newsroom. Among them was "Nelly Bly" the name of a popular song. Madden suggested she try it out. But one of the newspaper's printers made a mistake setting it into type.

And so Nellie Bly she became.

At that time proper American women wore several petticoats under their dresses, and white gloves in public. Teaching and nursing were the most advanced careers most women could hope for. The rough-and-tumble world of newspaper reporting was no place for a lady.

The few women reporters already employed covered events like flower shows and society balls. Nellie wasn't interested in those things. She wanted to cover the same stories as male reporters—hard news about politics or crime.

One area that drew her attention was business. In a big industrial city factories were everywhere. For example, Pittsburgh produced more than half of all the steel in the United States. Factories were dark, smelly, and dangerous. The workers worked twelve- or fourteen-hour shifts, six days a week. Recently unions had developed, organizing workers to improve their working conditions.

But the unions were not open to women.

Nellie Bly started a series of articles called "Our Workshop Girls," interviewing women at work. Nellie admired these women, many of whom were earning their independence as well as a weekly wage. They worked hard, and some were lucky enough to be paid fairly. But not every situation was a good one. Nellie found places where children were cruelly used. In others, workers were fined simply for talking while they worked.

Some factories, however, would not allow reporters inside. Naturally this only made Nellie more curious. What was happening behind the closed doors? Determined to find out, she pretended to be an unemployed working girl.

Her first stop was a basement workshop. She was hired to twist thin copper wires into thicker copper cables. It was one thing, Nellie discovered, to interview workers about their sore backs and aching eyes. It was quite another to feel these things for herself. After only an hour she was exhausted and thirsty. That's when she learned she couldn't even stop for a drink without asking her supervisor first.

Nellie openly shared her feelings and reactions with her readers. She brought the issue of the working poor to everyone's attention. "I work hard all day, week after week, for a mere pittance," she quoted one woman as saying. "I go home at night tired of labor, and longing for something new, anything good or bad, to break the monotony of my existence. I have no pleasure, no books to read. I cannot go to places of amusement for want of clothes and money, and no one cares what becomes of me."

These personal and emotional stories were unlike anything Pittsburgh had seen before. In just a few months Nellie's name was known all over town. Some people cheered her investigations. Others wanted her fired. And a few even proposed marriage.

Nellie never flinched. She was gaining confidence as fast as she was gaining experience.

She was no longer the shy girl who had arrived at the *Dispatch*'s offices hoping she was really supposed to be there. She was *Nellie Bly*, a real reporter and a name to be reckoned with.

CHAPTER THREE

A Mexican Adventure

AFTER HER SERIES on working girls was done, Nellie hoped to tackle other hard-hitting subjects. But her editor thought differently. He sent her to report on tree planting, new recipes and a new inconvenience called "hay fever." Nellie did what she told because she was still learning her trade. But she wasn't very happy. After a few months she quit the *Dispatch* staff.

Nellie badly wanted a change. "I was too impatient to work along at the usual duties assigned women on newspapers," she explained later, "so I conceived the idea of going away as a correspondent."

This idea had come to her after some Mexican officials had visited Pittsburgh. Nellie served on their entertainment committee, and though she spoke no Spanish, her enthusiasm and friendliness had made a good impression. She even received an invitation to come and visit Mexico.

Nellie was eager to go, but she wanted the *Dispatch* to send her. George Madden was doubtful. Mexico was an unstable country, he said. All the better—Nellie relished a chance for adventure. But she didn't know Spanish, Madden reminded her. That was true, but Nellie hadn't known Spanish when meeting with the Mexican officials, either. And finally, Madden pointed out, it wouldn't be safe for her to travel alone. Nellie had an answer for that too—her mother would also make the trip.

Knowing he was beaten, Madden gave in.

It was Nellie's first real trip to anywhere, and she found her preconceptions wrong from the start. "I had imagined that the West was a land of beef and cream," she wrote back to the *Dispatch* readers. "I soon learned my mistake, much to my dismay. It was almost an impossibility to get aught else than salt meat, and cream was like the stars—out of reach."

Once Nellie and her mother reached Mexico itself, they found a country of stark contrasts. There was great natural beauty and a rich culture. "A Sunday in Mexico is one long feast of champagne," Nellie noted, "without a headache the next day." On the other hand, she also wondered "why *pulgas* and *chinches* were ever invented. By the way, if it were not for their musical names they would surely be unendurable. There is a great deal in a name, after all, and if I had to call them fleas and bedbugs I should take the next train for the States."

There was also much poverty and violence. One town, just south of the border, seemed "to look with proud contempt on civilization and progress." The largest part of the population was "homeless, poor, uncared for, untaught . . . Their lives are hopeless, and they know it." There were also cooking habits to adjust to. Women tortilla makers, Bly noted, "spit on their hands to keep the dough from sticking"—and nobody seemed to mind.

Even among the poor, women held a lower position. Nor were they much respected. "It is considered polite and quite a compliment for a man to stare at a lady on the streets," she observed. "I might add that the men, by this rule, are remarkably polite."

And then there was bull fighting. Nellie marveled at its wide following even as she was disgusted by the spectacle. "At a fight two weeks ago one man was gored almost to death, another had his arm broken, and a woman, who had witnessed this from her seat, entered the ring and tried to kill the bull. She was caught on his horns and carried once around the ring and whirled round in her perilous position like a top. The audience shouted and was much disappointed when the bull cast the woman to the ground, devoid of clothing and badly bruised, but alive."

After the Mexican government jailed some dissenting newspaper editors, Nellie wrote an article criticizing the decision. In return she received a threatening message. "One button is enough," she was told, meaning she would be wise never to speak out like

that again. She would later write that "All the papers which I know of are subsidized by the government, and, until several months ago, they were paid to abstain from attacks on the government. . . . The Mexican papers never publish one word against the government or officials, and the people who are at their mercy dare not breathe one word against them, as those in position are more able than the most tyrannical czar to make their life miserable."

But for the moment she was careful. She had toured Mexican jails and had no desire to get a more permanent look.

After almost six months, it was time to go home.

CHAPTER FOUR

Welcome to New York

PITTSBURGH HAD ALWAYS been the biggest city in Nellie's life. But now that Nellie had done some traveling, Pittsburgh didn't look so big anymore. Of course, Nellie knew that Pittsburgh hadn't really changed in her absence.

She, however, had changed a lot.

Even getting a raise to fifteen dollars a week didn't help. The stories she was being offered were the same kind she had written before. After witnessing the grand people and places in her travels, it was a little hard to go back to discussing the latest style in hats.

And so, after a restless few months, Nellie packed her bags and moved to New York City—the busiest, most exciting city in America. She arrived there in the summer of 1887, determined to make a name for herself as soon as possible.

New York in the 1880s was a city bursting at the seams. Over a million people lived there already, and thousands more were arriving every week. There were elevated trains to carry them around, and buildings as tall as ten stories to work in. An invention called the telephone was becoming popular, and Thomas Edison's company was busy installing streetlights that ran on something called electricity. Out in the harbor the Statue of Liberty, less than a year old when Nellie arrived, had already settled into her new role greeting immigrants from Europe.

In such a colorful city New Yorkers had their choice of reading material. Seven or eight newspapers fought each day for their readers' attention. Their headlines screamed with dramatic scoops and announcements. Everything from government corruption to murders and mayhem were trumpeted in every edition.

One of the biggest of these papers was the *New York World*, owned by Joseph Pulitzer. Pulitzer had turned around the failing paper partly by championing the working class. It was the *World* that had started the campaign that had children sending in their pennies to help pay for the Statue of Liberty's base. Its daily circulation was 150,000, and its 309-foot tall headquarters was the tallest building in the world. And while Pulitzer's office on the top floor had leather-covered walls and a spectacular view, the *World* proudly declared that it would "always fight for progress and reform, never tolerate injustice or corruption."

Nellie knew the *World* would be perfect. They both shared a tendency toward plain speaking and an informal style. So she wrote to Pulitzer, introducing herself, and suggesting a couple of story ideas.

Pulitzer never wrote back. Nellie tried her luck with other editors, and they ignored her too. Nellie Bly might be a big name in Pittsburgh, but that was hundreds of miles away. Here in New York no one had ever heard of her. Even worse, she was in search of a job that most men didn't think a woman should have.

After four months of rejection, Nellie grew desperate. Her money was running out. And then her purse was stolen. With her patience and resources all but gone, she determined to make a final effort. She marched down to the *World*'s offices demanding to see the editor. Did she have an appointment, the guard asked? No, she didn't, Nellie replied, but she wanted to see the editor anyway.

"I at last gained admission," she recalled later, "by saying that I had an important subject to propose, and if the editor-in-chief would not see me, I would go to some other paper."

Impressed with Nellie's stubbornness, the managing editor, John Cockerill, finally asked her in for a meeting. He and Pulitzer listened as Nellie talked and talked. Despite their first misgivings, it was hard to ignore Nellie's passion and sense of commitment. They decided to advance her twenty-five dollars against payment for a story they had in mind. If the article turned out well, they would give her a job writing for the *World*.

Nellie was very pleased. All she wanted was a chance to prove herself. Now she was going to get it.

CHAPTER FIVE

Ten Days in a Madhouse

ON THE SURFACE Pulitzer's idea was simple enough. He wanted Nellie to pretend to be crazy. The reason was a little more complicated. At the time, people who were judged to be insane were taken away to special hospitals. How were they cared for? What chance did they have for recovery? No one was saying. Most of these people were never heard from again.

"I always had a desire," Nellie wrote afterward, "to know asylum life more thoroughly— a desire to be convinced that the most helpless of God's creatures, the insane, were cared for kindly and properly."

These asylums, though, were mysterious places hidden from the public. One of the biggest was Blackwell's Island Insane Asylum in the East River, just off of Manhattan. There were rumors that the patients inside were poorly treated, but such charges were hard to prove. And whenever an inspection was scheduled, the asylum staff always had plenty of warning to get things in order.

"We do not ask you to go there for the purpose of making revelations," Cockerill told her. "Write up things as you find them, good or bad; give praise or blame as you think best, and the truth all the time."

Nellie had a lot of confidence in herself, but even so, the assignment made her pause. "Did I think I had the courage to go through with such an ordeal as the mission would demand?" she wondered. "Could I assume the characteristics of insanity to such a degree that I could pass the doctors, live for a week among the insane without the authorities finding out?"

Still her determination remained strong. "I shuddered to think how completely the insane were in the power of their keepers, and how one could weep and plead for release, and all of no avail, if the keepers were so minded."

Her first step was to check into a boarding house. Nellie Brown, she called herself, just in case anyone had ever heard her name. She had only seventy-three cents in her pockets and claimed to have come from Cuba.

Nellie wasted no time making the other boarders feel uncomfortable. "They all look crazy," she announced. "I am afraid of them."

She sat in the parlor for hours, staring into space. "Everything was so sad," she remarked, to no one in particular. That night she refused to go to bed, afraid, she said, of what another tenant might do to her.

The next day the matron at the boarding house sent for the police. The police took her first to the local station and then to Bellevue Hospital. Nellie had worried about this part the most. Could she really fool the police and the doctors about her condition? Apparently she could. Both examined her, and both were only too willing to get her off their hands.

The hospital was cold and unfriendly. Dinner featured "a piece of boiled meat and a potato. It could not have been colder had it been cooked the week before, and it had no chance to make acquaintance with salt or pepper." She also had trouble sleeping:

"The bed was not a comfortable one. It was so hard, indeed, that I could not make a dent in it."

Soon she was transported by boat to the asylum. The conditions there were even worse than at the hospital. More importantly, the patients were treated with no respect or kindness. "If they talked they were scolded and told to shut up," she later wrote. "If they wanted to walk around in order to take the stiffness out of them, they were told to sit down and be still." Nellie encouraged the patients to tell the superintendent "how they were suffering . . . but they replied that the nurse would beat them if they told."

Her first night was especially uncomfortable. "I could not sleep, so I lay in bed picturing to myself the horrors in case a fire should break out in the asylum. Every door is locked separately and the windows are heavily barred, so escape is impossible."

As the days passed, Nellie observed the other patients closely. "They live, breathe, eat; the human form is there, but that something, which the body can live without, but which cannot exist without the body, was missing."

After the longest ten days of her life, a lawyer from the *World* arrived to get Nellie released. "I had looked forward so eagerly to leaving the horrible place. . . . I left the insane ward with pleasure and regret—pleasure that I was once more able to enjoy the free breath of heaven; regret that I could not have brought with me some of the unfortunate women who lived and suffered with me, and who, I am convinced, are just as sane as I was."

CHAPTER SIX

Reporter
at Large

"BEHIND ASYLUM BARS" proclaimed the headline of her story "Ten Days in a Mad-House" in the *New York World*. This was the first part of Nellie's series that ran on Sundays. By the time the second part, "Inside the Mad-House," was published a week later, Nellie Bly was all anyone was talking about.

The articles caused a sensation. Not only had Nellie documented how terribly patients were treated on Blackwell's Island, but she had done it from the inside—while pretending to be insane herself. No reporter, male or female, had ever tried such a stunt before. The outcry was immediate. The asylum conditions were investigated at once, and Nellie was called as a key witness. As she wrote, "I answered the summons with pleasure, because I longed to help those of God's most unfortunate children whom I had left prisoners behind me. If I could not bring them that boon of all boons, liberty, I hoped at least to influence others to make life more bearable for them."

When Nellie's charges, among others, were shown to be true, changes were ordered. Many of the worst nurses and other staff members were fired. And more money was sent to improve the asylum facilities.

The changes in Nellie's own life were dramatic as well. She was immediately hired by the *World* as a staff reporter. And just as it had in Pittsburgh, her writing immediately stood out. She wasn't a fancy writer, but she had a knack for drawing readers into a story, making them feel they were having the same adventure she was.

Nellie used this approach in several future assignments. In one, she visited employment agencies that specialized in finding jobs for working girls. Nellie pretended to be looking for a job herself. She found that the agencies were far better at collecting fees for registering the girls than they were at actually finding them work. She also found that an employment agency would change a girl's background or references in whatever ways were necessary to get her hired.

Another time Nellie investigated women who had turned to crime. She posed as one of these women herself in order to gain their confidence and hear their stories. Nellie rarely thought that women in a bad way had gotten there through their own faults. She blamed it on their lack of education or a difficult family situation.

One of her biggest triumphs took her to Albany, the New York state capital. A man named Edward R. Phelps lived there. He supposedly controlled many politicians, telling them how to vote in certain situations. In return the politicians received money from him in secret.

Although rumors of Phelps's actions had existed for years, no one had ever caught him in the act. But Nellie had a plan. A bill was pending in the New York legislature that would restrict the sale of some dangerous medicines. The medicine manufacturers were against this bill because it would be bad for their business. Nellie went to see Phelps at an Albany hotel, pretending to be the wife of one of these manufacturers. Her

husband's company would be ruined, she told him, if this bill became law. Wasn't there something he could do? She had $2000 available to help.

Phelps was taken in by her story. He bragged to Nellie that he could get any bill killed or passed. He showed her a list of politicians that he controlled. She appeared impressed. If he would give her a receipt, she would go and get her checkbook and strike a deal with him. Phelps gave her the receipt. Nellie took it, left the room—and never came back.

The front-page story titled "The King of the Lobby" exposed Phelps and many of the politicians he worked with. Others might still be in business, but they had been warned. With Nellie Bly snooping around, they would have to watch their step.

Through all of this, the *World* protected

Nellie's identity. They kept her description a secret so that she could go on doing her work without being recognized. Some people, however, didn't believe Nellie was a woman or even one reporter. No one person, they thought, could be so daring and resourceful. The *World* was happy about the mystery because it helped sell newspapers. And Nellie was happy, too, because she was doing exactly what she had always wanted to do.

CHAPTER SEVEN

Looking Ahead

NOT EVERYTHING NELLIE Bly wrote about was serious or grim. One time she described taking a ride in a hot air balloon. Another time she supposedly jumped off a ferry to see if the boat's rescue crew knew its job. She even tried dancing in a chorus line, making fun of herself first in front of the audience and later with her readers.

Nellie also did a lot of interviews, with people as varied as the jailed anarchist Emma Goldman and the boxing champion John L. Sullivan. She had a way of getting her subjects to relax, to think of her like a friend. "I have given you more," Sullivan confided to her, "than I ever gave any reporter in my life."

Most of the ideas that Nellie wrote about she came up with herself. "It was my custom," she explained, "to think up ideas on Sunday and lay them before my editor for his approval or disapproval on Monday."

But there came a Sunday when no ideas appeared, "and three o'clock in the morning found me weary and with an aching head tossing about in my bed." Tired and cranky, she suddenly blurted out, "I wish I was at the other end of the earth."

And why not? she thought. *I need a vacation; why not take a trip around the world?*

The idea pleased her. But whether she needed a vacation or not, she was still in search of a headline. And then she had a second inspiration: "If I could do it as quickly as Phileas Fogg did, I should go."

Phileas Fogg was the hero and main character of Jules Verne's novel *Around the World in Eighty Days*. The story tells how Fogg bets the members of his club that he can circle the globe in eighty days—a feat they consider impossible. Nevertheless, Fogg undertakes the trip—by train, boat, elephant, and hot air balloon. In the end he succeeds in his quest.

Nellie stepped almost shyly into the *World*'s offices the next morning. She had already checked the steamship schedules to see about a possible departure. But she wasn't sure how her editor would react to the idea.

"I want to go around the world," she blurted out. "I want to go around in eighty days or less. I think I can beat Phileas Fogg's record. May I try it?"

John Cockerill smiled. She was not the first to think of this idea, he told her. However, if anyone were to go, the paper assumed it would be a man. "In the first place," the editor explained later, "you are a woman and would need a protector, and even if it were possible for you to travel alone you would need to carry so much baggage that it would detain you in making rapid changes. Besides you speak nothing but English, so there is no use talking about it; no one but a man can do this."

But Nellie hadn't gotten as far as she had by meekly accepting such an answer. "Very well," she said angrily. "Start the man and I'll start the same day for some other newspaper and beat him."

Cockerill knew her well enough by now to understand that she wasn't bluffing. "I believe you would," he said slowly. And so after further negotiation, Nellie was assured that if the *World* sent anyone on a trip, it would send her.

And then for a year nothing more was said about it. But one wet evening Nellie received a note at home asking her to come to the office at once. This was most unusual. She arrived wondering whether she was in some kind of trouble. Instead, she was simply asked a question.

"Can you start around the world day after tomorrow?"

Of course she could. There were preparations to be made, naturally, and very little time to make them. She had a special dress made, one she could wear daily in many kinds of weather. She also decided to bring only one small piece of luggage—sixteen inches wide and seven inches tall. That way she would be as portable as possible if her connections demanded speed.

It was not a bag, though, that she filled lightly. "I was able to pack two traveling caps, three veils, a pair of slippers, a complete outfit of toilet articles, ink-stand, pens, pencils, and copy-paper, pins, needles, and thread, a dressing gown, a tennis blazer, a small flask and a drinking cup, several complete changes of underwear, a liberal supply of handkerchiefs . . . and a jar of cold cream to keep my face from chapping."

Although the *World* was booking her trip on well-established ships and trains, there was always the chance of danger, especially for a woman traveling alone. "Someone suggested that a revolver would be a good companion piece for the passport, but I had such a strong belief in the world's greeting me as I greeted it that I refused to arm myself."

And so, on Thursday, November 14, 1889, she stood on the deck of the *Augusta Victoria* at Hoboken Pier. And at 9:40 A.M., Nellie Bly started on her tour around the world.

CHAPTER EIGHT

A Trip around the World

NELLIE ADMITTED TO being a little nervous as her ship set sail. But outwardly she remained calm. As she had already reminded herself: "It's only a matter of 28,000 miles and seventy-five days and four hours, until I should be back again."

Her nervousness was understandable. Although Nellie was traveling on established routes, she could take little for granted. Many of her connections ran only once a week or even once a month. Missing just one could upset her whole timetable.

The *World* had heralded her departure

with several headlines including "Around the World! A Continuous Trip Which will Girdle the Spinning Globe." Everyone on the ship, from the captain to the lowest deckhand, knew why she was there. But now that the trip had begun, Nellie could only trust to fate. She could not make the ship's engine more efficient or put a strong wind at their backs. All she could do was watch and wait.

And get seasick. She was barely at sea before the first wave of nausea hit. She went straight to the railing, leaned over, and "gave vent to my feelings," as she put it. But after a long night and day spent mostly in bed, her stomach settled down nicely.

Her arrival in England came right on schedule. But there she had news of an unusual request. Mr. and Mrs. Jules Verne had invited her to come to dinner at their home as she passed through France. Would she do them that honor? Nellie was delighted. It would make things a little more hectic, but how could she refuse?

The Vernes were charming hosts. "Jules Verne's bright eyes beamed on me with interest and kindliness," Nellie wrote, "and Mme. Verne greeted me with the cordiality of a cherished friend." Verne asked about the route she had planned. After England and France, she explained, she would pass through Italy by train before boarding a series of ships that would take her to Egypt, Aden, Ceylon, Malaya, Hong Kong, Japan, and back to the United States.

The Vernes were encouraging about her journey, if a bit skeptical about her chances of success. "If you do it in seventy-nine days, I shall applaud with both hands," Jules Verne told her.

After her train rides across France and

Italy, Nellie boarded another ship, the *Victoria*. Its route would take her through the Mediterranean Sea and down through the recently opened Suez Canal. Unfortunately her accommodations on this ship weren't quite as nice as they had been on the *Augusta Victoria*. "Travelers who care to be treated with courtesy and furnished with palatable food," she wrote back to her readers, "will never by any chance travel on the *Victoria*."

There was also the proud father in the next cabin who rose early each day to ask his young daughter a question. "What does the moo-moo cow say, darling; tell papa what the moo-moo cow says?" Nellie quickly tired of this. "If it had been once, or twice even, I might have endured it with civilized forbearance but after it had been repeated . . . for six long weary mornings, my temper gave way. I shouted frantically: 'For heaven's sake, baby, tell papa what the moo-moo cow says and let me go to sleep.'

"The fond parents did not speak to me after that."

Despite her six months in Mexico, Nellie hardly considered herself a widely experienced traveler. Still, she had the advantage over one young bride, whom she overheard talking about the ship. "Yes, everything is very nice," the young woman commented, "but the life preservers are not quite comfortable to sleep in."

Once through the Red Sea, the *Victoria* continued on to Ceylon. There Nellie had to wait five days for her next connection.

Ceylon was beautiful. There were plants and flowers unlike anything she had ever seen. Other local attractions included a local snake charmer. As Nellie described it,

he "began to play on a little fife, meanwhile waving a red cloth which attracted the cobra's attention. It rose up steadily, darting angrily at the red cloth, and rose higher at every motion until it seemed to stand on the tip end of its tail."

Even half way around the world, though, she could not resist poking a little fun at things back home. "I have spoken about the perfect roads in Ceylon. I found the roads in the same state of perfection in almost all the Eastern ports at which I stopped. I could not decide, to my own satisfaction, whether the smoothness of the road was due to the entire and blessed absence of beer wagons, or to the absence of New York street commissioners."

Although Nellie had packed lightly, she was interested in collecting remembrances from the trip. The most notable of these was the street monkey she bought in Singapore. McGinty, as he was later called, became her traveling companion for the second half of her journey.

So far the weather had been fairly cooperative. But as Nellie moved toward Hong Kong her ship was caught in a great monsoon. Great waves crashed over the ship, filling even the passenger cabins with water. Nellie was undaunted. She stated that she "would rather go in dead and successful than alive and behind time."

In Hong Kong she received disturbing news. It seemed she was now in a race. The magazine *Cosmopolitan* had sent another female reporter, Elizabeth Bisland, to travel around the world too but in the opposite direction. And so far it appeared that Bisland was ahead.

Nellie was not pleased, but she could do

nothing about it. But as she took ship for Japan, it was hard to think that all of her hard work might be wasted.

She felt better upon leaving Yokohama, still on schedule after almost two months away. Nellie appreciated the chance to catch her breath after years of constant activity. "To sit on a quiet deck, to have a star-lit sky the only light above or about, to hear the water kissing the prow of the ship, is, to me, paradise," she wrote while crossing the Pacific.

Another succession of storms, though, slowed her ship's progress. Nellie began to think that perhaps she would miss the record, after all. It was a hard fact to accept. But the ship's captain, aware of her goal, increased the ship's speed to make up the lost time.

Her arrival in San Francisco set off a

triumphant cross-country train ride. She made many stops along the way, and sometimes thousands of well-wishers turned out to cheer her on. Nellie wasn't just reporting the news anymore. She was making it. On January 25, 1890, she arrived at the train station in Jersey City, New Jersey—72 days, 6 hours, 11 minutes after her departure. It was a new world record. (As for Elizabeth Bisland, she had bad luck in her connections and turned out to be no threat at all.)

A huge crowd was waiting for Nellie, and a cannon broadside marked the moment. The sight of so many people moved her deeply. They shouted out their congratulations, and she responded in kind. "I took off my cap and wanted to yell with the crowd, not because I had gone around the world in seventy-two days, but because I was home again."

CHAPTER NINE

Moving
On

NELLIE BLY WAS now famous. She wasn't just famous in New York City or even in the United States. She was famous all over the world. Every newspaper ran stories about her and her remarkable feat. And she was no longer anonymous, either. Her photograph had been published far and wide along with her story. Many people, though, found it most remarkable that a woman had traveled around the world with only one piece of baggage in tow.

Always practical, Nellie expected some kind of bonus for all of her hard work. The

World had profited handsomely on their investment in the trip. They had not only published her reports on the front page, they had run a contest—"Your Nellie Bly Guessing Match"—asking readers to predict how long the journey would take. With so much publicity, more New Yorkers were buying the newspaper than ever. And advertisers were eager to pay higher prices to reach them.

Nellie felt entitled to share in the rewards. But Pulitzer and the other editors, while pleased with her success, offered her no bonus or special gift to honor her achievement.

Unhappy and disappointed, Nellie decided to take a break from reporting. She resigned from the *World* and went on a speaking tour. She also had her adventures published. The book was her third, after *Ten*

Days in a Mad-House and *Six Months in Mexico.* It was called *Nellie Bly's Book: Around the World in 72 Days.* She ended it with a special thank you. "To so many people this wide world over am I indebted for kindnesses. . . . To each and all of you, men, women, and children, in my land and the lands I visited, I am most truly grateful."

Nellie enjoyed being the center of attention, but as much as she liked traveling and sharing stories about her experiences, these things were in the past. And Nellie was someone who always looked ahead. So in 1893, when a new editor at the *World* invited her to return to the staff, she accepted the chance.

Nellie had the freedom to choose her own stories, but she also had more competition around town. The situation had changed in three years. Both the *World* and other newspapers were hiring women to do some of the same things Nellie had pioneered. But her strength was still making readers feel like they were at her side. She also moved easily from one kind of topic to another. She wrote about spending a night in a supposedly haunted house, exposing a scheme to con money from wealthy women, and working with charitable Salvation Army volunteers.

Her biggest story was covering the Pullman strike in 1894. George Pullman was the inventor of the sleeping train car, and these railroad cars were built in his own factory town outside of Chicago. His workers did more than just earn their living from Pullman. They bought food and clothing at his stores and rented rooms in his boarding houses.

It was widely thought that the workers were well treated. Pullman was supposedly a generous employer. The workers didn't agree, especially after he cut their wages but left the salaries of his managers untouched.

To go on strike—to disrupt a business by refusing to work—was a new idea. Businesses were naturally against it. They pictured strikers as mean and unruly, ready to fight anyone who disagreed with them. As a result soldiers had been called in by Pullman to maintain order.

Reporters flocked to the town from everywhere, and Nellie Bly was among them. She didn't think well of strikes because she thought they only hurt the workers. After all, Mr. Pullman was not going to go hungry, no matter how long the workers sat on their hands.

"I came to Chicago bitterly set against the strikers," Bly said in her column. "I thought the inhabitants of the model town of

Pullman hadn't a reason on earth to complain. With this belief I visited the town, intending in my articles to denounce the rioters and bloodthirsty strikers."

It didn't take her long to see things differently. From a distance the town seemed pretty and well kept. But away from the main street, the model town was not so model. Cramped and dirty quarters were everywhere.

"Before I had been half a day in Pullman," Nellie wrote, "I was the most bitter striker in the town."

She not only wrote a story sympathizing with the strikers, she went off to see the governor of Illinois and tell him what she had seen.

Other newspapers were careful not to be critical of Pullman because he represented big business. But Nellie always spoke her

mind. In the end the strike was not settled as peacefully as she would have liked, but her readers got a truer picture of what had really happened.

Epilogue

REPORTING WAS THE heart and soul of Nellie Bly's life. She took in a situation, sized up people quickly, and then charged straight ahead. She wasn't one to waste a lot of time weighing her choices.

So it wasn't really surprising when she got married in 1895 only a few days after meeting her future husband. He was Robert Seaman, a millionaire industrialist. Seaman was many years older than Nellie, but they got along well from the start.

Some people wondered about the marriage, but Nellie just ignored them and moved on. She gave up her reporting pencil once more and settled into married life. After her husband's death ten years later, she took up the job of running his company. But the mixture of caring and daring that had worked in reporting didn't serve her interests so well in the world of business, and the company failed.

Settling the company's affairs left Nellie without much money. She went to Europe for a rest—and arrived just in time for the start of World War I. She spent the next few years reporting on events there before returning home in 1919.

Even in her fifties Nellie was still writing stories, looking out for anyone too poor or powerless to look out for themselves. But it took her death in 1922 to remind people of how much she had accomplished. Her scoops and exposés were significant not simply because she happened to be a woman but because she brought a refreshing viewpoint to the nature of reporting. It was said at the time that a good newspaper should afflict the comfortable and comfort the afflicted. Nellie Bly would have agreed. She always made it her business to do just that.

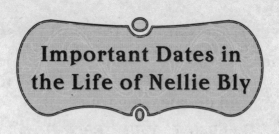

Important Dates in the Life of Nellie Bly

1864 Born May 5 as Elizabeth Cochran in Cochran's Mills, Pennsylvania

1870 Death of her father, Michael Cochran

1879 Finishes schooling without graduating high school Adds "e" to her last name around this time

1885 Starts working as a reporter for the Pittsburgh *Dispatch*

1886 Travels to Mexico as a correspondent for the *Dispatch*

1887 Moves to New York City

Begins working at *New York World* after writing series about the ten days she spent in an asylum

Publishes *Ten Days in a Mad-House* about the experience as a series in the *World*, as well as a book

1888 Publishes *Six Months in Mexico*

1890 Travels around the world in seventy-two days

Leaves the *New York World* to write and do speaking tours

Publishes *Nellie Bly's Book: Around the World in 72 Days*

1893 Returns to the staff of the *New York World*

1895 Marries Robert Seaman

1904 Takes control of Seaman's company, Iron Clad Manufacturing, after his death

1913 Loses control of Iron Clad Manufacturing after company goes bankrupt

1914–7 Writes about World War I for *New York Evening Journal*

1919 Comes back to the United States, continues to write

1922 Dies January 27 from pneumonia

Bibliography

Bly, Nellie. *Six Months in Mexico*. New York: John W. Lowell, 1886.

Bly, Nellie. *Nellie Bly's Book: Around the World in Seventy-Two Days*. New York: Pictorial Weekly, 1890.

Bly, Nellie. *Ten Days in a Mad-House*. New York: Norman L. Munro, 1887.

Burrows, Edwin G. and Wallace, Mike. *Gotham: A History of New York City to 1898*. New York: Oxford University Press, 1999.

Ehrlich, Elizabeth. *Nellie Bly*. New York: Chelsea House, 1989.

Kroeger, Brooke. *Nellie Bly: Daredevil, Reporter, Feminist*. New York: Random House, 1994.

Peck, Ira, ed. *Nellie Bly's Book: Around the World in Seventy-Two Days*. Brookfield, CT: Millbrook Press, 1998.

Swanberg, *W. A. Pulitzer*. New York: Charles Scribner's Sons, 1967.

About the Author

STEPHEN KRENSKY is the author of more than sixty fiction and nonfiction books for children, many of them with a historical theme. When he feels he has spent enough time hunched over his computer, he likes to play tennis and softball. He lives in Lexington, Massachusetts, with his wife, Joan, and their two sons.